20 RECIPES KIDS SHOULD KNOW

RECIPES + TEXT BY ESME WASHBURN (AGE 12)

PHOTOGRAPHS BY CALISTA WASHBURN (AGE 17)

PRESTEL

MUNICH + LONDON + NEW YORK

CONTENTS

INTRODUCTION

I have loved cooking ever since I can remember. I first learned how to cook from my grandma, who also loves to cook. She started teaching me when I was really little, and many of my favorite memories are of cooking with her. As I got older, I started to read cookbooks from cover to cover, as if I was reading a chapter book. In order to get inspiration for all different types of dishes, I checked out tons of cookbooks from the library. As I read more cookbooks, however, I started to notice that many of the cookbooks made for kids consisted of random recipes for snacks and sweets and didn't actually teach you how to make a meal. I decided to create this book so that all kids can learn basic recipes that are not only fun and easy, but that also teach you important cooking skills and techniques. Enjoy!

WEIGHTS AND MEASUREMENTS

For measuring dry and solid ingredients, spoon the ingredient into the measuring cup or spoon, and use a knife or straight edge to "level it off," to knock off anything that goes over the top. Do not push down any ingredient into the cup, except for brown sugar, which should always be firmly packed.

For measuring liquid ingredients, pour the liquid to the line of the amount needed, let the measuring cup sit on a flat surface, and position your eyes at the level of the line in order to make sure the liquid is exactly at the line.

IMPORTANT MEASUREMENTS

1 stick of butter = ½ cup = 8 tablespoons =
4 ounces = 113 grams
2 sticks of butter = 1 cup = 227 grams
4 sticks of butter = 1 pound = 454 grams

3 teaspoons = 1 tablespoon = 15 milliliters
4 tablespoons = ¼ cup = 60 milliliters
8 tablespoons = ½ cup = 120 milliliters
12 tablespoons = ¾ cup = 180 milliliters

1 liquid cup = 8 ounces = 235 milliliters
2 liquid cups = 16 ounces = 470 milliliters
1 pint = ½ quart = .47 liter
2 pints = 1 quart = 0.95 liter
4 quarts = 1 gallon = 3.8 liters
16 ounces = 1 pound = 454 grams

SAFETY TIPS

- Make sure you ask a parent or adult for permission before you use the stove, oven, knives, or any other hot or sharp tools.

- Always wash your hands before and after you touch food.

- If you touch raw meat, fish, or eggs, make sure you wash your hands before you touch anything else and you thoroughly wash anything that touched it so that you do not spread germs around your kitchen. It is a very good idea to get different cutting boards for different uses. I have ones for raw meat, vegetables, onions and garlic, and bread and cheese.

- When using a knife or sharp tool, always have a parent or adult supervise you and help you while you cut.

- When you cut something, curl your fingertips in and hold the food with your knuckles down so that you don't cut your fingers.

- NEVER cut when your or someone else's fingers or any other body parts are on the cutting board!

- Make sure to use pot holders or oven mitts whenever you move hot pots and pans.

BEFORE YOU START COOKING…

- Tie back your hair and roll up long sleeves.
- Read the recipe through fully.
- If you don't want to get dirty, put on an apron.
- Wash your hands.
- Make sure the surfaces that you are using are clean.
- Make sure you have all of your ingredients.
- Wash your fruits and veggies.

AFTER YOU FINISH COOKING…

- Put away all the ingredients that you used.
- Clean and put away all the pots, bowls, utensils, etc. that you used.
- Wipe down all surfaces.

GLOSSARY/COOKING TECHNIQUES

TO BEAT: To mix vigorously, usually using a whisk, spoon, spatula, or stand mixer.

TO BLEND OR PURÉE: To make a smooth liquid by grinding or mashing something, usually a fruit, vegetable, sauce, or soup, typically using a food processor or blender.

TO BOIL: To heat a liquid in a pot or pan until it bubbles with big bubbles that rise rapidly.

TO CHOP: To cut something, usually a vegetable, into smaller pieces.

In order to chop an onion, cut off the top and bottom of the onion, and peel off the papery outer layers. Stand the onion up on one of the cut ends and cut it in half vertically. Take one onion half, and cut many vertical slices. Turn the onion ninety degrees, and cut many horizontal lines, to make many small cube-shaped pieces.

TO CREAM: To mix butter and sugar together until it is light and fluffy.

Begin by beating softened butter in a bowl. Add the sugar and continue to beat until the mixture lightens in color and is fluffy.

TO DICE: To chop into small, approximately ⅛-inch (3 mm) cubes.

TO FOLD: To mix something into a batter without stirring, typically using a spatula or spoon.

In order to fold, use a spatula or spoon to cut a line through the center of the batter. Then, move the spatula to one side of the line in order to scrape the bottom of the bowl. Bring the spatula upward along the side of the bowl, turn the bowl 90 degrees, and repeat until it is fully mixed in.

TO GRATE: To shred something, typically cheese or crunchy vegetables, using a grater.

TO KNEAD: To work a dough in order to make it more elastic. In order to knead a dough, spread a thin layer of flour on a clean table or work surface. Put the dough on the work surface and, using the heel of one hand, push down and forward 2 to 3 times, folding it in half after each time. Rotate the dough 90 degrees, fold it in half, and repeat. Continue this until the dough is a smooth, elastic ball.

TO MINCE: To cut something, typically garlic or herbs, into extremely small pieces.

In order to mince garlic, separate a clove from the garlic head, lay it on its side, and lay the flat side of a knife with a large blade on top of it. Carefully use the heel of your hand to press the blade downwards in order to crush the garlic clove. Remove the papery outer skin of the garlic, and then use the blade of the knife to chop the garlic into very small pieces.

TO SAUTÉ: To cook food, usually vegetables, in a pan with a little oil or butter.

TO SIMMER: To heat a liquid in a pot or pan on low heat so that it has small, slow-rising bubbles.

TO STIR: To mix gently using a circular motion.

TO WHIP: To beat something, usually egg whites or cream, really hard in order to incorporate air into it.

TO WHISK: To mix thoroughly using a whisk.

In my family, there is a huge debate about which are the best pancakes—thick and fluffy pancakes or thin, crêpe-like pancakes. I'm including both a classic, thinner pancake recipe and a fluffier buttermilk version, adapted from Marilyn Covey's recipe in her book, Right Off the Farm, and pictured at right. They are both delicious! For the classic pancake recipe, you can reduce the milk to make thicker pancakes and increase the milk to make thinner pancakes. I like to add blueberries, thinly sliced banana, or even chocolate chips to my pancakes immediately after I pour the batter. Serve the pancakes with butter and real maple syrup or fruit (strawberries and bananas) and whipped cream.

PANCAKES TWO WAYS

PREP TIME: 10 MINUTES ✕ **COOKING TIME: AROUND 2½ TO 3½ MINUTES PER BATCH** ✕ **SERVES 4 TO 6**

INGREDIENTS

FOR CLASSIC PANCAKES

2 large eggs

2¼ **CUPS** (540 ml) milk, plus more as needed

3 **TABLESPOONS** salted butter, melted (2 tablespoons canola or vegetable oil can also be used)

2 **CUPS** (260 g) all-purpose flour (or 1½ cups / 195 g all-purpose flour and ½ cup / 65 g whole wheat flour can also be used)

1 **TABLESPOON** sugar (optional)

1 **TEASPOON** baking powder

¼ **TEASPOON** baking soda

2 **TEASPOONS** ground cinnamon or vanilla extract (optional)

FOR BUTTERMILK PANCAKES

2 large eggs

2½ **CUPS** (600 ml) buttermilk

¼ **CUP** (60 ml) canola or vegetable oil

2 **TEASPOONS** vanilla extract

2 **CUPS** (260 g) all-purpose flour (or 1 cup / 130 g all-purpose flour and 1 cup / 130 g whole wheat flour)

2 **TEASPOONS** baking powder

¾ **TEASPOON** baking soda

½ **TEASPOON** fine sea salt

DIRECTIONS

1 In a large bowl, whisk together the eggs, milk or buttermilk, butter or oil, and vanilla extract, if using.

2 In a medium bowl, whisk together the flour(s), sugar, if using, baking powder, baking soda, cinnamon, if using, and salt, if using. Make sure the dry ingredients are thoroughly mixed together.

3 Add the dry ingredients to the wet ones, and stir with a large spoon until just combined. It is fine for the batter to have lumps. Do not overmix.

4 Let the batter rest for at least 5 minutes.

5 Heat a griddle (or a heavy-bottomed frying pan) over medium heat. It is essential to evenly heat the griddle before making the first pancake, but the griddle should not be too hot. (You can test this by sprinkling a little water on the griddle. If the water sizzles and evaporates soon after it touches the griddle, the temperature is just right. If the water evaporates with lots of steam right when it touches the griddle, the griddle is too hot!) Carefully grease the griddle with canola or vegetable oil.

6 Using a large spoon, pour the batter onto the hot griddle to make 4 to 8 pancakes. The batter thickens as it sits, so add more milk to the classic pancake batter, as needed. Do not overmix, and do not add extra milk to the fluffy pancake batter!

7 Cook the pancakes until little bubbles start to form on the surface, 1 to 2 minutes.

8 Using a spatula, carefully flip the pancakes only once and cook until the second side is golden brown, about another 1 to 2 minutes. Note: The buttermilk pancakes cook around 1 minute longer than the classic pancake.

9 Remove the pancakes with a spatula and serve immediately. Repeat with the remaining batter, greasing the griddle as needed.

What do you do with overripe bananas? I like to bake banana bread. This easy recipe makes a moist banana bread that stays fresh for several days. I like to make it on Sundays, so I can have it for breakfast during the week, or as an after-school snack. Unfortunately, my sisters often devour it right away. I like to use a combination of whole wheat and all-purpose flours, but if you only have all-purpose flour that is fine. Usually, I add chocolate chips to the bread, but it's also great plain or with dried cranberries and/or walnuts.

ULTIMATE BANANA BREAD

PREP TIME: 25 MINUTES × **COOKING TIME: 50 TO 75 MINUTES** × **MAKES 1 (9-INCH / 23 CM) LOAF / SERVES 8**

INGREDIENTS

½ **CUP** (115 g) salted butter (1 stick), at room temperature

¾ **CUP** (150 g) sugar

3 to 4 very ripe bananas, peeled (approximately 1¾ cups / 525 g)

2 large eggs

1½ **TEASPOONS** vanilla extract

2 CUPS (260 g) all-purpose flour (a combination of 1½ cups / 195 g all-purpose flour and ½ cup / 65 g whole wheat flour can also be used)

1 TEASPOON baking soda

½ **TEASPOON** baking powder

½ **CUP** (120 ml) plain whole milk yogurt (nonfat, low-fat, or vanilla yogurt can also be used)

1 TABLESPOON canola or vegetable oil

1 CUP (175 g) chocolate chips (optional)

⅔ **CUP** (95 g) dried cranberries (optional)

¾ **CUP** (90 g) chopped walnuts (optional)

NOTE: The banana bread is best eaten as soon as it is cool, but it also keeps well. Wrap the bread in foil and keep at room temperature for up to 3 days or refrigerate for about a week. Banana bread can also be well wrapped and frozen for up to 3 months.

DIRECTIONS

1 Preheat the oven to 350°F (180°C). Butter the bottom and sides of a 9-inch (23 cm) loaf pan. Lightly dust the pan with flour, tapping out any excess.

2 In a large bowl, beat the butter with a large spoon until soft and creamy. Slowly add the sugar and continue beating until light and fluffy with a smooth and uniform texture, 1 to 2 minutes.

3 In a small bowl, mash the bananas with a fork until smooth but still chunky. Add the mashed bananas to the butter mixture and stir until well combined.

4 Add the eggs, 1 at a time, and mix well. Add the vanilla extract and mix thoroughly.

5 In a medium bowl, whisk together the flour, baking soda, and baking powder. Make sure the dry ingredients are thoroughly mixed together. Gradually add the dry ingredients to the wet ones, and stir with a large spoon until just combined. Do not overmix.

6 Add the yogurt and oil and stir until just blended. Again, do not overmix.

7 Fold in the chocolate chips, dried cranberries, and/or chopped walnuts, if using.

8 Pour the batter into the prepared loaf pan. Bake until the top is golden brown and a toothpick or skewer inserted in the crack that forms at the top comes out clean, 50 to 75 minutes. (If the top is browning too quickly, tent the pan with aluminum foil.) Start checking the bread at 50 minutes. It may bake an extra 5 to 25 minutes longer, depending on how many bananas you use.

9 Remove the bread from the oven and let cool in the pan set on a wire rack for 10 minutes. Carefully remove the bread from the pan, place it directly on the wire rack, and let cool for 1 hour before slicing.

I think eggs make the perfect meal, because they are both filling and delicious. When I am not rushing to get to school, I make myself an omelet for breakfast—it's slightly more complicated to make than scrambled eggs, but so tasty! My family prefers cheddar cheese, but you could add any cheese that you like. If it's too hard to fold the omelet in half, you can also put the cheese in a line down the center of the omelet and fold both sides in towards the middle line of cheese in order to make a more rectangular version. The key to a good omelet is to butter the pan very generously so the eggs don't stick. I usually just make cheese omelets, but you can add other ingredients if you like such as bacon, tomatoes, and/or peppers.

CLASSIC CHEESE OMELET

PREP TIME: 5 MINUTES ✕ **COOKING TIME: 3 MINUTES** ✕ **MAKES 1 OMELET / SERVES 1**

INGREDIENTS

2 large eggs

1 TABLESPOON heavy cream

Fine sea salt

Ground black pepper

1 TABLESPOON unsalted butter

⅓ **CUP** (30 g) grated cheddar cheese

DIRECTIONS

1 Crack the 2 eggs into a small bowl.

2 Add the heavy cream and a pinch of salt and pepper to the eggs. Whisk until the mixture is a uniform yellow color with no streaks of egg white or yolk.

3 Heat a medium (10-inch / 25 cm) skillet over medium heat. When the pan is very hot (after about 30 seconds), add the butter and tilt the pan to coat the entire bottom with butter. Heat the butter until fully melted and sizzling. Do not let the butter brown.

4 Lower the heat to medium. Slowly add the eggs and tilt the pan so that the eggs cover the entire bottom.

5 Using a fork, make many small, circular stirring motions to briefly scramble the eggs in each part of the pan. If any gaps form, tilt the pan slightly so the liquid egg fills the hole. Stop stirring once the egg starts to become firm or jelly-like so you do not break the omelet. Once scrambled, let the omelet cook until it is no longer runny, about 10 seconds.

6 Place the cheese in a semicircle on half of the omelet.

7 Continue to cook the omelet until it is just set but not hard, and the cheese is almost fully melted, about 20 seconds.

8 Using a spatula, gently fold the half of the omelet without cheese over the half with cheese so the cheesy part of the omelet is covered. Remove from the heat and let the omelet sit in the pan for about 15 seconds.

9 Using the spatula, slide the omelet out of the pan and onto a plate. Serve warm, with your favorite toast, like the one on page 45.

There are two types of mac and cheese: stovetop and baked. I prefer this stovetop recipe, which starts with a flour and butter mixture called a roux and then uses milk to create a creamy béchamel sauce. I use cheddar cheese, which I think has the perfect mixture of creaminess, tanginess, and saltiness. You can also use Gruyère or another aged, sharp cheese that melts well or even a combination of cheeses. This mac and cheese is rich and creamy, but I could still eat it every day!

CREAMIEST MAC AND CHEESE

PREP TIME: 5 MINUTES ✕ **COOKING TIME: 25 MINUTES** ✕ **SERVES 4 TO 6**

INGREDIENTS

- **1 POUND** (454 g) pasta (rotelle, penne, farfalle, cavatappi, orecchiette, or elbows)
- **4 TABLESPOONS** (55 g) salted butter (½ stick)
- **¼ CUP** (33 g) all-purpose flour
- **2 CUPS** (480 ml) whole milk (low-fat or nonfat milk can also be used), at room temperature
- **14 OUNCES** (400 g) grated sharp cheddar cheese (approximately 4⅔ cups)
- **½ TEASPOON** salt (or to taste)
- **¼ TEASPOON** ground black pepper
- Grated Parmigiano-Reggiano cheese (optional)
- Pinch of chili flakes (optional)

DIRECTIONS

1 Fill a large pot with water and a large pinch of salt and bring to a boil. Add the pasta and cook according to the package directions until al dente, about 8 to 10 minutes.

2 While the pasta is boiling, make the béchamel sauce: In a 3-quart (2.8 l) heavy-bottomed saucepan over low heat, melt the butter. Add the flour while whisking constantly and cook until a smooth paste forms, about 2 minutes—this is the roux.

3 Continue whisking and slowly add the milk, 1 tablespoon at a time. When you have added 6 tablespoons (90 ml) of milk, the sauce should start to be smooth with a batter-like consistency. Continue to slowly whisk in the remaining milk. This takes about 8 to 10 minutes total.

4 Increase the heat to medium and continue whisking until the sauce comes to a boil and starts to thicken, about 3 minutes. After the sauce thickens, reduce the heat back to low and add the cheddar cheese, whisking constantly to make sure there are no lumps.

5 Drain the pasta and reserve ¼ cup (60 ml) of the pasta water.

6 Add the cooked pasta to the béchamel sauce and stir with large spoon until the pasta is completely coated in sauce. Continue cooking over low heat for 2 to 3 minutes. If the sauce gets too thick, add a little pasta water as needed. Add the salt, to taste, and the pepper. Mix in the Parmigiano-Reggiano cheese and chili flakes, if using, and serve.

NOTE: If you have any leftovers, you can store them in an airtight container in the refrigerator for up to 3 days and reheat in a pan over low heat, adding a few tablespoons of milk and stirring gently but constantly until heated through.

Grilled cheese sandwiches are a classic. They are fast to make and they are always delicious! The key to a really good grilled cheese is using bread that doesn't have any large holes that the cheese can fall through. It's also important to evenly coat the bread with butter, which helps create an even, golden brown color. Sourdough bread is usually really good for grilled cheese. I love using cheddar cheese, but you can use Swiss, Gruyère, Monterey Jack, mozzarella, or any other cheese that melts well. You can also add slices of tomato, bacon, or any other toppings you want. It's usually easiest to cook the sandwich first, let it cool for a minute, and then separate the slices of bread and add your topping.

QUINTESSENTIAL GRILLED CHEESE SANDWICH

PREP TIME: 5 MINUTES ✕ **COOKING TIME: 5 TO 6 MINUTES** ✕ **MAKES 1 SANDWICH / SERVES 1**

INGREDIENTS

About 2 ounces (57 g) cheddar cheese

2 thick slices of bread

2 **TABLESPOONS** salted butter, softened

DIRECTIONS

1 Heat a griddle, cast-iron skillet, or any heavy-bottomed pan over medium-low heat.

2 Cut the cheese into slices that are approximately ¼-inch (5 mm) thick. If you have larger pieces of bread, you may need more cheese, and if you have smaller pieces of bread, you may need less.

3 Arrange an even layer of cheese on 1 slice of bread and place the other slice of bread on top of the cheese to make a sandwich.

4 Spread 1 tablespoon of the butter on the top of the sandwich so that it coats the bread evenly, but you can still see the bread's texture. You might not need to use all of the butter.

5 Flip the sandwich over and butter the other side with the remaining 1 tablespoon of butter.

6 Place the sandwich on the griddle or in the pan. It should be hot enough that the sandwich sizzles gently.

7 Cover the pan with a lid and cook the sandwich until the bottom slice of bread is golden brown and the cheese starts to melt, 2 to 3 minutes.

8 Use a spatula to flip the sandwich. Cover the pan again and cook until the cheese is completely melted and the other slice of bread is golden brown, 2 to 3 minutes. Use a spatula to transfer the sandwich to a plate and enjoy!

Every time I visit my grandmother, I get so excited when I see her cooking black bean soup. This is the perfect soup for any bean lover, and even if you don't like black beans, this soup will change your mind! Although this recipe only has a few ingredients, it is incredibly flavorful and has a great texture, which is a result of combining puréed and whole beans. I like making a large batch of this soup on the weekends, because it is even more delicious reheated during the week. This soup is delicious by itself, but it's also great garnished with fresh cilantro, sliced avocado, corn tortilla chips, and/or a little sour cream.

TASTY BLACK BEAN SOUP

PREP TIME: 5 MINUTES ✕ **COOKING TIME: 60 TO 90 MINUTES** ✕ **MAKES 8 CUPS / SERVES 8**

INGREDIENTS

1 POUND (454 g) dried black beans

1 medium yellow onion, cut into quarters or chunks

2 TEASPOONS fine sea salt

1 chipotle chile in adobo or 1 teaspoon chipotle powder or hot sauce (optional)

OPTIONAL GARNISHES:

Fresh cilantro, sliced avocado, corn tortilla chips, sour cream

DIRECTIONS

1 Rinse the beans in a colander and place them in a large pot with a lid.

2 Add the onion quarters or chunks and bury them in the beans.

3 In a medium pot, bring about 8 cups (2 l) of water to a boil. Turn off the heat and carefully pour the boiling water over the beans until the water is 1 inch (2.5 cm) above the beans. Turn the heat to high and bring the water, beans, and onion to a boil, about 2 minutes. Reduce the heat to low and let the water, beans, and onion simmer.

4 Add the salt and chipotle chile, if using. (You can use a whole chile, for a bit more smoky spice flavor, or just a teaspoon of the sauce if you want slightly less spice—or you can use both!)

5 Continue simmering the beans until they are soft and you can squish them, 60 to 90 minutes. (The cooking time depends on the freshness of the beans.)

6 With a slotted spoon, remove about half of the beans and set aside in small bowl.

7 Transfer the remaining beans, onion, chile, and any liquid in the pot to a blender and purée until smooth. (You can also use an immersion blender or a food processor; you can even use a potato masher, if you mash it very well!)

8 Return the reserved whole beans and the puréed beans to the pot and bring to a simmer over medium heat. Taste the soup and add more salt or chipotle chile to suit your taste buds. If the soup is a little too thick, add more water. Serve hot.

NOTE: The soup can be stored in an airtight container in the refrigerator for several days. It will thicken slightly over time, so add a small amount of water when reheating to get the consistency you like.

I love hummus. It's healthy, delicious, and the perfect snack for when I come home from school. Many people buy their hummus premade, but it's very easy to make at home and it tastes much, much better when you do! I like to add a pinch of cayenne pepper to make the flavor a bit more complex, but not enough to make it spicy. My sister loves her hummus with extra olive oil, so if you like it that way, you can add a few more tablespoons to the recipe. I like serving it with pita chips and fresh vegetables like carrots, bell peppers, and radishes. You can also eat it with soft pita bread or a flour tortilla.

HEAVENLY HUMMUS

PREP TIME: 5 MINUTES ✕ **MAKES 1⅓ CUPS (315 ML)**

INGREDIENTS

2 CUPS (330 g) canned chickpeas, rinsed and drained

1 large clove garlic, minced

¼ CUP (60 ml) tahini

¼ CUP (60 ml) extra-virgin olive oil, plus more for drizzling

3 TABLESPOONS freshly squeezed lemon juice

¼ TEASPOON fine sea salt

Pinch of cayenne pepper (optional)

2 tablespoons water

DIRECTIONS

1 In a food processor or blender, combine the chickpeas, garlic, tahini, olive oil, lemon juice, salt, and cayenne, if using.

2 Add 2 tablespoons water and blend until very smooth, about 2 minutes.

3 Serve chilled or at room temperature. Drizzle with more olive oil and sprinkle with more cayenne pepper, if desired.

NOTE: You can store the hummus in an airtight container in the refrigerator for up to 1 week. I like to add a thin layer of olive oil on top to help preserve freshness.

This salad dressing is excellent on all kinds of lettuce. It's especially good on red and green leaf lettuce, romaine, kale, and arugula (also known as rucola or rocket), which is my personal favorite. I make sure to eat some greens every day and this salad makes a great addition to just about every meal. You can also add vegetables (like carrot, cucumber, tomato, and avocado), cheese (like Parmigiano-Reggiano or cheddar), and/or a protein (like grilled strips of chicken or steak) and eat it as a full meal in itself! My family likes to drizzle toasted sesame oil and soy sauce on it right before serving, but it is also delicious just by itself.

GREEN SALAD WITH DELICIOUS DIJON DRESSING

PREP TIME: 5 MINUTES ✕ **SERVES 2 TO 4**

INGREDIENTS

2 TEASPOONS Dijon mustard

2 TABLESPOONS red-wine vinegar

1 TEASPOON balsamic vinegar

Pinch of fine sea salt and additional salt to taste

¼ **CUP** (60 ml) extra-virgin olive oil

4 CUPS (80 g) of your favorite salad greens

Ground black pepper (to taste)

Shaved Parmigiano-Reggiano cheese (optional)

DIRECTIONS

1 In a jar or any small container with a lid, combine the Dijon mustard, vinegars, and salt and shake until mixed thoroughly.

2 Add the olive oil and shake again until mixed well. (The oil will come to the top, but don't worry about that!)

3 Thoroughly rinse your greens and dry in a salad spinner or using a clean tea towel.

4 Arrange the greens in a large bowl. Shake the dressing again and drizzle about 2 tablespoons over the greens.

5 Toss the salad with two spoons or other serving implements. Season to taste with coarse salt and pepper, as needed. Sprinkle with the shaved cheese, if using, and serve!

NOTE: Leftover dressing can be stored in a jar or any small container with a lid and refrigerated for up to 1 week. Be sure to bring the dressing to room temperature and shake it vigorously before using.

There are many excellent ways to prepare chicken, but this recipe is a favorite. When I was little, my babysitter used to make breaded chicken for my older sisters and me. Breading the chicken and cooking it in a skillet gives it a nice, crispy texture that we all love. As I got older, I started making this dish myself, substituting panko for the breadcrumbs. Panko is a Japanese-style breadcrumb that's especially light and flaky. Both panko and regular breadcrumbs work well, but I really love how crisp and airy the chicken crust is with panko. I typically use thin-cut chicken breasts for this recipe, because they cook faster and make for a good breading-to-chicken ratio. I like serving them with lemon slices and my sisters like dipping them in ketchup. We all love to eat this chicken with mashed potatoes and roasted vegetables or salad.

CRISPIEST BREADED CHICKEN

PREP TIME: 5 MINUTES × **COOKING TIME: 6 MINUTES** × **SERVES 4**

INGREDIENTS

½ **CUP** (65 g) all-purpose flour

1 large egg

¾ **CUP** (60 g) panko breadcrumbs
(or regular breadcrumbs)

1 TEASPOON fine sea salt

½ **TEASPOON** ground black pepper

4 pieces thin-cut boneless, skinless
chicken breast or cutlets

2 TABLESPOONS canola or
vegetable oil, plus more if needed

NOTE: You can substitute the chicken
with a white fish, such as cod, tilapia,
or sole. The cooking time is about
the same.

DIRECTIONS

1 Put the flour, egg, and breadcrumbs in 3 separate shallow bowls.

2 Whisk the egg until it is a uniform yellow color with no streaks of egg white or yolk.

3 Add the salt and pepper to the breadcrumbs and stir until mixed thoroughly.

4 Place each piece of chicken in the flour and turn to coat in a thin layer of flour.

5 Dip and flip each flour-coated piece of chicken in the egg mixture so that it is completely covered with egg.

6 Place each egg-coated piece of chicken in the breadcrumb mixture and turn to completely coat in breadcrumbs.

7 Heat a cast-iron skillet or any heavy-bottomed pan over medium-high heat.

8 Add the oil and heat until a drop of egg sizzles when added to the pan. If you are using a large pan, you might need to use extra oil.

9 Add the chicken and cook, flipping once, until golden brown all over, 2 to 3 minutes per side. If you use thicker pieces of chicken, you will need to cook it for longer. Add extra oil to the pan between batches as needed.

10 Remove the chicken from the pan and let it sit in a paper towel to remove excess oil.

This steak is another family favorite. We love using flank steak, because it's flavorful and has a good amount of fat, but you can use whichever type of steak you like best (skirt or hanger are good substitutes). I love including soy sauce and toasted sesame oil in my marinade. The soy sauce adds saltiness, enhances the meaty flavor of the steak, and helps tenderize it. The sesame oil gives it greater complexity. If you don't have double black soy sauce, which is richer in flavor because it contains molasses, you can use more of the regular soy sauce (or tamari) in its place. For the cooking and cutting parts of this recipe, steps 4 to 7, I recommend having an adult help you.

MOUTHWATERING MARINATED STEAK

PREP TIME: 5 MINUTES (PLUS 30 MINUTES TO 4 HOURS FOR MARINATING) × **COOKING TIME: 6 TO 8 MINUTES** × **SERVES 4 TO 6**

INGREDIENTS

1 **TABLESPOON** extra-virgin olive oil

2 **TABLESPOONS** soy sauce or tamari

1 **TABLESPOON** Chinese double black soy sauce

1 **TABLESPOON** toasted sesame oil

1½ **to** 2 **POUNDS** (680 to 900 g) steak, preferably flank steak

4 **TEASPOONS** coarse ground black pepper

½ **TEASPOON** coarse sea salt

DIRECTIONS

1. In a 9 x 13-inch (23 x 32.5 cm) baking dish, combine the olive oil, soy sauce, double black soy sauce, and sesame oil.

2. Add the steak to the baking dish and flip to coat both sides in the marinade. Sprinkle the salt and pepper evenly on both sides of the steak.

3. Cover the baking dish with plastic wrap or aluminum foil and put it in the refrigerator to marinate for at least 30 minutes or up to 4 hours.

4. Heat a cast-iron skillet (or any other heavy-bottomed pan) over high heat until it is very hot. The pan may start to smoke, but it's important to get it really hot, so let it heat for about 5 minutes and have an adult help you turn on the fan above the stove or open a window to help with any smoke.

5. Add the steak to the pan and cover with a large lid. Cook, flipping once, about 3 minutes per side for medium, depending on the thickness of the steak. If using a thermometer, cook the steak until it reaches an internal temperature of 140°F (60°C) for medium; the temperature will rise to about 145°F (63°C) while the steak rests.

6. Remove the steak from the skillet, cover with a lid or foil tent, and let rest for 10 minutes. (Letting the steak rest prevents all of the juices from running out of the meat when you cut it, resulting in a more juicy steak.)

7. Cutting across (perpendicular to) the grain (the long lines in the meat), cut the steak into thin strips.

Who doesn't love pizza? Our family has always had one favorite dinner ritual—Sunday night pizza. We used to order pizza, but then realized it's even more delicious and so much fun to make it at home where everyone can customize an individual pie with different toppings. I've experimented with a lot of pizza dough recipes, and what I love about this pizza dough is that it can be ready within an hour, but still has a great taste and is easy to handle. As for toppings, you can add just about anything you want to your pizza. Sliced peperoni, browned Italian sausage, diced onions, garlic, and sliced bell peppers all work well. I'm a pizza purist and love a classic margherita pie, but I also love pesto pizza. Yum!

PERFECT PIZZA

PREP TIME FOR PIZZA DOUGH: 15 MINUTES ✕ **RISING TIME FOR DOUGH: 45 MINUTES** ✕ **PREP TIME: 5 MINUTES PER PIZZA** ✕
COOKING TIME: 3 TO 5 MINUTES PER PIZZA ✕ **MAKES 6 (8- TO 10-INCH / 20 TO 25 CM) PIZZAS**

INGREDIENTS

FOR THE DOUGH

2 (¼-ounce / 7 g) packages active-dry yeast

1½ CUPS plus 2 tablespoons (385 ml) warm water

4 CUPS (520 g) all-purpose flour

3 TABLESPOONS extra-virgin olive oil

1 TABLESPOON coarse sea or kosher salt

2 TEASPOONS sugar

2 TABLESPOONS cornmeal for dusting (optional)

FOR THE TOPPINGS

¾ to 1¼ CUPS (180 to 295 ml) Tomato Sauce or Pesto (pages 30–31)

15 OUNCES (425 g) mozzarella cheese, preferably fresh

2 TABLESPOONS (30 ml) extra-virgin olive oil

Coarse sea salt or kosher salt to taste

1½ cups (85 g) grated Parmigiano-Reggiano cheese (optional)

Fresh basil leaves, for serving (optional)

DIRECTIONS

MAKE THE DOUGH

1 In a stand mixer fitted with a dough hook attachment, or in a large bowl, combine the yeast and warm water then add the flour, olive oil, salt, and sugar.

2 Using the dough hook, mix the ingredients on low for 2 minutes. Increase the speed to medium and knead until the dough is smooth and elastic, about 1 to 2 minutes. Form the dough into a ball. You can also knead the dough by hand; see step 5 in the recipe for Back to Basics Bread (page 45) for kneading instructions.

3 Put the dough in a clean medium bowl that's been lightly oiled with vegetable or canola oil. Cover the bowl with a clean, damp tea towel (or plastic wrap). This prevents the dough from getting a hard crust while it rises. Let the dough rise at room temperature for 30 minutes.

4 Divide the dough into six equal portions and shape each portion into a round ball. Place the balls of dough on a lightly floured work surface, cover with the damp tea towel, and let sit for 15 minutes.

MAKE THE PIZZA

1 Preheat the oven to its highest setting, usually 550°F (285°C). Place a pizza stone or baking sheet on the middle rack of the oven and let it heat up for 5 minutes.

2 Dust a pizza peel or large cutting board with cornmeal or flour. Using your fingers and knuckles, gently stretch a ball of dough into an 8- to 10-inch (20 to 25 cm) circle and place on the prepared pizza peel.

3 Spread 2 to 3 tablespoons of tomato sauce or pesto evenly on the dough using the back of a spoon. Tear 2 ½ ounces (70 grams) of mozzarella into small (roughly 1-inch / 2.5 cm) pieces and scatter over the tomato sauce. Add toppings, if desired. Drizzle with 1 teaspoon (5 ml) of olive oil and sprinkle with a pinch of salt to taste.

4 With the help of an adult, slide the dough onto the pizza stone in the oven. Bake until the crust is lightly brown and the cheese is bubbling, 3 to 5 minutes.

5 Remove the pizza from the oven and cool for 1 minute. Top with Parmigiano-Reggiano and basil, if using, and serve whole or cut into quarters.

When my sisters and I were very young, the first thing our grandmother taught us to make was fresh pasta. You might think it's hard to make or that you need special equipment, but it's actually really simple. This recipe can be made into all different shapes—you can even make ravioli with it—but I love cutting the dough thin and making fettucini. This pasta is so good by itself that you can just add butter and grated Parmigiano-Reggiano cheese. In summer, there is nothing better than making a fresh tomato sauce or pesto, but you can make those sauces in other seasons, too. I use canned tomatoes except when they are in season. Of course, you can also use these sauces with dried pasta, if you aren't able to make it fresh—just follow the cooking instructions on the package. They're both delicious on any kind of pasta.

FRESH PASTA WITH TOMATO SAUCE OR PESTO

PREP TIME: 30 MINUTES (PLUS 30 MINUTES FOR CHILLING) PLUS 5 TO 15 MINUTES FOR THE SAUCES ×
COOKING TIME: 3 MINUTES FOR FRESH PASTA PLUS 30 MINUTES IF MAKING TOMATO SAUCE × SERVES 4

INGREDIENTS

FOR THE PASTA

2 **CUPS** (260 g) all-purpose flour, plus more as needed

2 large eggs

1 **TABLESPOON** extra-virgin olive oil

1 **TABLESPOON** salted butter

Grated Parmigiano-Reggiano cheese, for serving (optional)

FOR THE TOMATO SAUCE

¼ **CUP** (60 ml) extra-virgin olive oil

1 small onion, finely diced

1 clove garlic, finely minced

1¾ **POUNDS** (795 g) fresh tomatoes or 1 (28-ounce / 795 g) can peeled plum tomatoes

1 **TEASPOON** fine sea salt

½ **TEASPOON** ground black pepper

½ **TEASPOON** sugar, plus more as needed

Fresh basil leaves, for serving (optional)

FOR THE PESTO SAUCE

2½ **CUPS** (80 g) fresh basil leaves

¼ **TEASPOON** salt (plus more to taste)

1 clove garlic

⅓ **CUP** (44 g) pine nuts (pignoli)

½ **CUP** (125 ml) extra-virgin olive oil

4 **OUNCES** (114 g) Parmigiano-Reggiano cheese, cut into roughly 10-inch cubes (approximately ¾ cup)

DIRECTIONS

MAKE THE PASTA

1 Place the flour in a mound on a clean work surface and use your fingertips to make a well in the center.

2 Break the 2 eggs in the center of the well. **PHOTO A. SEE ILLUSTRATIONS ON NEXT 2 PAGES**

3 Add the olive oil to the eggs and mix them together with a fork or your fingertips. **PHOTO B** Gradually bring the flour into the egg and oil mixture using your fingertips or a bench scraper, which makes mixing easier.

4 Gather the flour and shape the dough into a ball, adding drops of water if the dough is too crumbly or a little extra flour if it's too sticky. (The dough should be a bit dry but not crumbly or sticky).

5 Once the dough comes together into a ball and is not falling apart, knead it by pushing the heel of your hand down into the dough and folding the dough over. Continue kneading until the dough is smooth and soft and stretchy, 5 to 10 minutes. **PHOTO C**

RECIPE CONTINUES ON FOLLOWING SPREAD

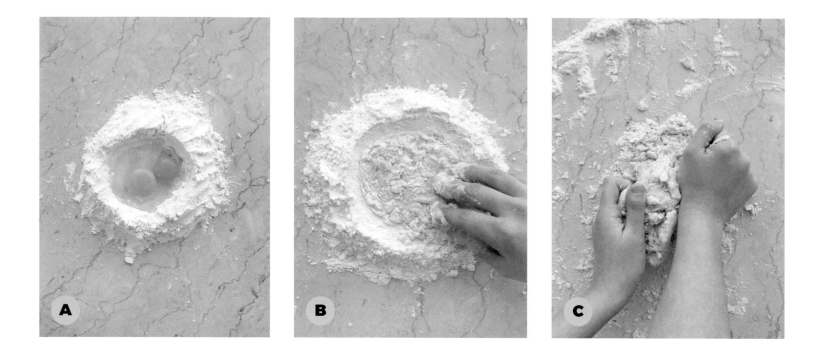

6 Cover the dough with a large bowl, a damp tea towel, or plastic wrap and let it sit for 30 minutes.

7 After 30 minutes, cut the dough into quarters. Leave 3 of the quarters covered and place the fourth on a clean work surface. Using a rolling pin, roll out the dough, flipping it and turning it to keep it even, until it's thin enough that you can just about see your hand through it, 5 to 10 minutes. The rolled dough should roughly be in the shape of a long rectangle. You can very lightly flour the dough, and the work surface, if needed. **PHOTO D**

8 Once you have finished rolling out the dough, carefully roll it into a long, loose cylinder. Be sure to roll and not fold the dough. Repeat with the remaining dough so you have 4 cylinders of dough.

9 Cut the rolled-up cylinders of dough into ⅛-inch (2.5 mm) to ¼-inch (5 mm) thick strips (or whatever width you prefer) and quickly unravel them. **PHOTO E** Gently shake the strips of pasta so they don't stick together, very lightly flour them, and shape into little nests using your fingers. Place the nests of pasta on a baking sheet, plate, or tray covered with a tea towel, while you make the tomato sauce or pesto. **PHOTO F**

NOTE: The fresh pasta can be stored in an airtight container in the refrigerator for 24 hours or frozen for 1 to 2 months.

MAKE THE TOMATO SAUCE

1 In a heavy-bottomed frying pan, heat the olive oil over medium heat. Add the onion and sauté, stirring often with a spoon or fork, until soft and translucent, about 4 minutes.

2 Add the garlic and sauté until very fragrant, about 30 seconds. Do not let the garlic brown.

3 Place the tomatoes and any extra liquid in a medium bowl and use your hands to gently crush them. Add to the onion mixture in the frying pan.

4 Add the salt, pepper, and sugar and simmer, occasionally stirring and scraping around the sides of the frying pan with a rubber spatula, until the tomato sauce thickens and is no longer watery, about 20 minutes. Taste the sauce (let it cool first) and add more salt, pepper, and sugar as needed. (I prefer a thicker, chunkier sauce, but if you like a smoother sauce, or want to use the sauce for pizza, pureé it in a blender or food processor.)

NOTE: The tomato sauce is best served immediately, but you can store it in an airtight container in the refrigerator for up to 3 days. You can also store it in the freezer for up to 6 months.

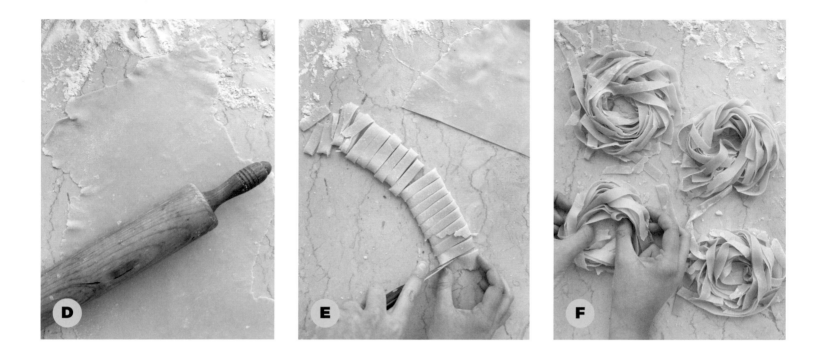

MAKE THE PESTO

1 In a food processor or blender, combine the basil leaves, salt, and garlic and blend until finely minced, about 30 seconds. Then, using a spatula, scrape down the sides.

2 In a small, preferably cast-iron pan, toast the pine nuts over medium heat until they turn lightly brown, about 2 minutes. Watch the pine nuts carefully so they don't burn.

3 Add the pine nuts to the food processor and blend until well combined, about 30 seconds. Scrape down the sides again if necessary.

4 With the food processor running, slowly pour in the olive oil, blending until the mixture is very smooth.

5 Add the Parmigiano-Reggiano and blend until fully combined and smooth.

NOTE: The pesto can be stored in an airtight container with a thin layer of olive oil on top for up to 1 week in the refrigerator. You can also store it in the freezer for a couple of months, but if you're going to freeze it, do not add the cheese until after you thaw the pesto. I like to freeze small amounts of pesto in ice cube trays.

TO SERVE

1 Fill a large pot with water and add a teaspoon of salt and bring to a boil. Add the pasta and cook until al dente, 2 to 3 minutes.

2 Drain the pasta and reserve ¼ cup (60 ml) of the pasta water. Pour the cooked pasta back into the pot.

3 Add the butter and 1 tablespoon of the reserved pasta water to keep the pasta from getting too dry.

4 Add the tomato sauce or pesto and toss to combine. Add the grated Parmigiano-Reggiano and basil, if using, and serve.

In my family, mashed potatoes have always been a Thanksgiving-only type of food. Recently, though, we have started eating them more often throughout the year. They are quite easy to make, and they are so fun to mash! I include a little Parmigiano-Reggiano cheese in my recipe, because it gives the mashed potatoes a depth of flavor and saltiness that I love, but you could definitely add cheddar or any other hard, aged cheese that you like. If you want, you can also skip the cheese, but you might need to add a little extra salt. These mashed potatoes are a little chunky. I like them this way, but you can mash them more if you prefer a smoother texture.

AMAZING MASHED POTATOES

PREP TIME: 15 MINUTES ✕ **COOKING TIME: 30 TO 40 MINUTES** ✕ **SERVES 6 TO 8**

INGREDIENTS

- **3 POUNDS** (1.4 kg) russet potatoes (about 5 medium-large potatoes)
- **1½ TEASPOONS** coarse sea salt, divided (plus more to taste)
- **6 TABLESPOONS** (85 g) salted butter, at room temperature
- **¼ CUP** (60 ml) whole milk, at room temperature
- **4 OUNCES** (113 g) cream cheese, at room temperature
- **1 TEASPOON** ground black pepper (plus more to taste)
- **¾ CUP** (180 ml) heavy cream, at room temperature
- **¼ CUP** (20 g) grated Parmigiano-Reggiano cheese (optional)

DIRECTIONS

1 Peel the potatoes and cut them into equal-size quarters.

2 Put the potatoes in a large pot. Add 1 teaspoon of the salt and enough water to cover the potatoes by about 2 inches (5 cm). Bring to a boil over medium-high heat. Reduce the heat and simmer until the potatoes feel soft when you stick them with a fork, 20 to 30 minutes.

3 Turn the heat off and drain the potatoes. Place the potatoes back in the pot and add the butter. With a fork or potato masher, mash the potatoes until the potato pieces are broken up into smaller pieces.

4 Turn the heat to medium-low, add the milk and cream cheese, and continue mashing until the potatoes are creamy, but still have a chunky texture, about 5 minutes. Do not overmix.

5 Add the remaining ½ teaspoon salt and the pepper. If you are going to serve the mashed potatoes right away, add the heavy cream and Parmigiano-Reggiano, if using, and keep cooking 2 to 3 more minutes.

NOTE: If you do not plan to serve the mashed potatoes immediately, wait to add heavy cream and Parmigiano-Reggiano until you're reheating for serving. You can reheat them in a saucepan on medium-low heat.

People are often surprised when I tell them how much I like Brussels sprouts, but roasting gives them such an incredible flavor and crispy texture. I love roasting lots of different vegetables because it makes them even more delicious! Keep in mind that different vegetables cook at different rates (see note below). I like my roasted veggies crispy, but you can cook them as little as 20 minutes or as much as an hour for large root vegetables. You can roast one kind of vegetable or choose from a combination of your favorite vegetables.

CRISPY ROASTED VEGETABLES

PREP TIME: 15 MINUTES ✕ **COOKING TIME: 20 TO 60 MINUTES (DEPENDING ON THE VEGETABLE)** ✕ **SERVES 4**

INGREDIENTS

½ to 2 POUNDS (225 to 905 g) your choice of vegetables (I usually use either broccoli [½ pound / 225 g], asparagus [1½ pounds / 680 g], carrots [2 pounds / 905 g], or Brussels sprouts [1½ pounds / 680 g])

3 TABLESPOONS extra-virgin olive oil

1½ TEASPOONS coarse sea salt

Ground black pepper

DIRECTIONS

1 Preheat the oven to 400°F (200°C).

2 Wash and dry the vegetables with a tea towel. Make sure they are completely dry. See the exact preparation for each vegetable in the note below.

3 Spread the vegetables out on a baking sheet. Drizzle with the olive oil and sprinkle with the salt. Using your hands, toss the vegetables to make sure they are coated with oil. Carefully spread them out so that they don't overlap on the sheet.

4 Roast for 10 minutes and then carefully flip the vegetables over and roast until tender on the inside and crispy on the outside, 10 to 30 minutes, depending on the vegetables. You can roast the vegetables longer if you prefer them more crisp. Season to taste with salt and pepper and serve.

PREPARATION AND APPROXIMATE ROASTING TIMES FOR VEGETABLES

ASPARAGUS: Break off the tough, bottom end and leave whole; roast 20 to 25 minutes (tender, but still crisp).

BROCCOLI: Peel the stalk and cut off the florets, leaving about 2 inches (5 cm) of the stalk attached to each floret; cut each piece lengthwise, so each looks like a half-tree; roast 20 minutes (tender, but crispy on the edges and slightly browned).

BRUSSELS SPROUTS: Trim off the bottom stubs and cut in half lenghtwise; roast 35 to 40 minutes (crispy and slightly browned).

CARROTS: Trim off carrot tops and leave carrots whole if thin or halve lengthwise if thick; roast 30 to 60 minutes depending on thickness (tender and browned).

FENNEL: Cut off the stalks and the root, slice the bulbs in half lengthwise, and cut into 1-inch (2.5 cm) wedges; roast 40 minutes (soft and slightly browned and caramelized edges).

GREEN BEANS: Break off the tips and leave whole; roast 20 minutes (slightly shriveled and browned in spots).

SWEET POTATOES: Peel and cut into ¼-inch (6 mm) discs; roast 30 to 45 minutes (tender and slightly browned).

My sisters and I have always loved watching Ina Garten's cooking show and reading her cookbooks. This recipe was originally from Garten's The Barefoot Contessa Cookbook, but I have tweaked it a little bit over time. The cake is very moist and super chocolaty. I like to use Dutch-process cocoa powder (like Droste), which creates a deep chocolate flavor. To contrast all that chocolate, I recommend using a vanilla cream cheese frosting—you won't even know there is cream cheese in it, but it cuts the sweetness and perfectly complements the rich, chocolate cake. This is my go-to cake for birthday parties and any special event!

BEST CHOCOLATE CAKE EVER!

PREP TIME: 30 MINUTES ✕ **COOKING TIME: 25 TO 30 MINUTES** ✕ **SERVES 8 TO 10**

INGREDIENTS

FOR THE CHOCOLATE CAKE

1¾ **CUPS** (228 g) all-purpose flour, plus more for dusting

1 **CUP** plus 1 tablespoon (240 g) Dutch-process cocoa powder

1½ **TEASPOONS** baking soda

½ **TEASPOON** baking powder

¾ **CUP** (170 g) salted butter (1½ sticks), at room temperature, plus more for greasing

⅔ **CUP** (135 g) granulated sugar

⅔ **CUP** (145 g) firmly packed light brown sugar

2 large eggs

2 **TEASPOONS** vanilla extract

1 **CUP** (240 ml) buttermilk

½ **CUP** (120 ml) plain whole milk yogurt (nonfat, low-fat, or vanilla yogurt can also be used)

2 **TABLESPOONS** brewed coffee, preferably decaffeinated (optional)

FOR THE CREAM CHEESE FROSTING

½ **CUP** (115 g) salted butter (1 stick), at room temperature

8 **OUNCES** (226 g) cream cheese, at room temperature

About 3½ **CUPS** (350 g) confectioners' sugar

1 **TABLESPOON** heavy cream, plus more as needed

1 **TABLESPOON** vanilla extract

DIRECTIONS

MAKE THE CAKE

1. Preheat the oven to 350°F (180°C). Line 2 (8-inch / 20 cm) round pans with parchment paper. Butter the paper and the sides of the pans. Lightly dust the pans with flour, tapping out any excess.

2. In a medium bowl, whisk together the flour, cocoa powder, baking soda, and baking powder. Make sure the dry ingredients are thoroughly mixed together.

3. In a large bowl, beat the butter with a large spoon or 3-pronged fork until soft. Slowly add the granulated and light brown sugars and continue beating until light and fluffy with a smooth and uniform texture, 2 to 5 minutes. (You can also use a hand mixer or a stand mixer.) Add the eggs, 1 at a time, and vanilla and mix well.

4. In a small bowl, combine the buttermilk, yogurt, and coffee and mix well.

5. Alternate adding ⅓ of the flour mixture and ⅓ of the buttermilk mixture to the butter mixture, mixing until just combined. Do not overmix.

6. Pour the batter evenly into the prepared pans. Bake until a toothpick or skewer inserted in the cake comes out clean, 25 to 30 minutes.

7. Remove the cakes from the oven and set on a wire rack. Let cool in the pans for 10 minutes. Carefully remove the cakes from the pans, place directly on the wire rack, and let cool completely before icing.

NOTE: The cake and frosting can be made a day in advance of assembling. Wrap the cake in plastic wrap and refrigerate the frosting in an airtight container. The assembled cake can be covered and stored in the refrigerator for 3 to 4 days. Serve at room temperature.

MAKE THE FROSTING

In a large bowl, beat the butter and the cream cheese by hand using a large spoon until soft and creamy, about 1 minute. Add the confectioners' sugar and heavy cream and continue beating until smooth. Add vanilla and beat until the frosting has a smooth and spreadable consistency. If the frosting is too stiff, add a bit more heavy cream.

ASSEMBLE THE CAKE

Place one cake layer on a plate with the flat side facing up and ice the top with frosting. Place the second cake layer, flat side facing up, on top of the frosted layer and ice the top. Ice the sides of the cake, cut, and serve.

I have been adjusting, tweaking, and experimenting with this recipe for a few years in order to come up with the perfect chocolate chip cookie—one that has great flavor and is chewy (or bendy, as we say in my family) and not too thick or too thin. I like to use 60% cacao chocolate chips because dark chocolate is delicious in cookies. I prefer chips slightly larger, but any chocolate chips will work. It is fun and easy to make this recipe by hand, but you can use an electric or stand mixer, if you prefer. Although everyone in my family likes a different style of chocolate chip cookie, we can all agree that these are delicious!

CHEWY CHOCOLATE CHIP COOKIES

PREP TIME: 20 MINUTES ✕ **COOKING TIME: 12 TO 15 MINUTES PER BATCH** ✕ **MAKES 36 (3-INCH / 7.5 CM) COOKIES**

INGREDIENTS

1 CUP (2 sticks / 226 g) salted butter, at room temperature

½ **CUP** (100 g) granulated sugar

1¼ **CUPS** (275 g) firmly packed light brown sugar

2 large eggs

2 **TEASPOONS** pure vanilla extract

2 **CUPS** (260 g) all-purpose flour

½ **TEASPOON** baking powder

½ **TEASPOON** baking soda

¼ **TEASPOON** salt, preferably kosher salt

1⅔ **to 2 CUPS** (10 to 12 ounces / 285 to 340 g) bittersweet chocolate chips

NOTE: The cookies are best enjoyed as soon as they are cool, the day they are made, but can be stored in an airtight container for up to 3 days.

DIRECTIONS

1 Preheat the oven to 325°F (160°C). Line a baking sheet with parchment paper or a silicone baking mat.

2 In a large bowl, beat the butter with a large spoon until soft and creamy. Slowly add the granulated and light brown sugars and continue beating until light and fluffy, 1 to 2 minutes.

3 Add the eggs to the butter mixture and beat for about 1 minute. Add the vanilla and beat until smooth, about 30 seconds.

4 In a medium bowl, whisk together the flour, baking powder, baking soda, and salt. Make sure the dry ingredients are thoroughly mixed together.

5 Gradually add the flour mixture to the dough, stirring just until the dough comes together, about 1 minute. (You can also use a stand mixer on medium speed just until the ingredients are well combined, about 30 seconds.) Do not overmix. Fold the chocolate chips into the dough with a spatula or large spoon.

6 Transfer the dough to an airtight container, or cover with plastic wrap, and refrigerate for about 30 minutes. (The dough can be refrigerated overnight or up to 1 week.)

7 Roll the dough into heaping 1 tablespoon mounds and arrange in 3 rows of 4 on the prepared baking sheet. The cookies will spread, so leave about 2 inches (5 cm) in between the mounds of dough. Slightly flatten each mound of dough with clean fingers, or the back of a spoon, and make sure the chips are evenly distributed.

8 Bake for 7 minutes then rotate the baking sheet and continue baking until the edges of the cookies are slightly brown and the tops are just set, about 5 to 8 more minutes.

9 Remove the cookies from the oven and let cool on the baking sheet, set on a wire rack, for about 5 minutes. Using a spatula, place the cookies directly on the wire rack and let cool completely. Repeat with the remaining dough to make more cookies.

Strawberries are only in season for a short time, but when they are, I make strawberry shortcake as often as possible. Even when strawberries are not in season or not available, I still make strawberry shortcake using frozen berries, which are picked and frozen in season, so they taste great anytime. These biscuits are adapted from Cook's Illustrated magazine. They're fast and easy and come out consistently well each time. These biscuits are also delicious just with butter and jam!

SUPER STRAWBERRY SHORTCAKE

PREP TIME: 20 MINUTES ✕ **COOKING TIME: 15 MINUTES** ✕ **MAKES 8 TO 10 (3-INCH / 7.5 CM) BISCUITS; SERVES 8 TO 10**

INGREDIENTS

FOR THE BISCUITS

2 **CUPS** (260 g) all-purpose flour

1 **TABLESPOON** baking powder

2 **TEASPOONS** sugar

½ **TEASPOON** fine sea salt

1½ **CUPS** (360 ml) heavy cream

FOR THE STRAWBERRIES

1½ **POUNDS** (680 g) fresh strawberries

2 **TABLESPOONS** sugar

FOR THE WHIPPED CREAM

1½ **CUPS** (360 ml) heavy cream

1 **TABLESPOON** sugar

2 **TEASPOONS** vanilla extract

DIRECTIONS

MAKE THE BISCUITS

1 Preheat the oven to 400°F (200°C). Line a baking sheet with parchment paper.

2 In a large bowl, whisk together the flour, baking powder, sugar, and salt. Make sure the dry ingredients are thoroughly mixed together.

3 Add the heavy cream and stir until the dough is almost fully together, about 30 seconds.

4 Place the dough on a lightly floured work surface and knead for about 30 seconds.

5 Using a rolling pin, roll out the dough until ¾ to 1 inch (2 to 2.5 cm) thick. Be sure to rotate the dough every couple of rolls and to lightly flour the work surface as needed to prevent sticking. Don't use too much flour!

6 Using a 3-inch (7.5 cm) round cookie cutter, cut the dough into 8 to 10 biscuits. Be sure to just press straight down and do not twist the cutter. Pull away any excess dough then reroll it and cut more biscuits.

7 Place the biscuits on the lined baking sheet. Bake for 7 minutes then rotate the baking sheet front to back and continue baking until just golden brown, about 8 more minutes.

8 Remove the biscuits from the oven and, using a spatula, place the biscuits directly on a wire rack and let cool slightly, about 5 minutes.

WHILE THE BISCUITS ARE BAKING, PREPARE THE STRAWBERRIES

1 Rinse the strawberries thoroughly. Cut off the green tops then cut the strawberries into quarters and place in a medium bowl.

2 Add the sugar to the strawberries and stir. (If the strawberries are in season and very sweet, you don't need to add sugar.) With a fork, in the same bowl, crush about a quarter of the strawberries. Let sit while making whipped cream.

NOTE: Extra biscuits can be enjoyed on their own—they are delicious with butter. They can also be wrapped in a double layer of plastic bags and frozen for up to 2 months.

MAKE THE WHIPPED CREAM

In a large bowl, use a large whisk to beat together the heavy cream and sugar. Add the vanilla extract and keep beating until the cream thickens and soft peaks form.

ASSEMBLE THE SHORTCAKES

Split the cooled biscuits in half and place the bottoms on individual plates. Spoon a generous amount of strawberries on top of the biscuit bottoms and top with a small amount of whipped cream. Add the biscuit tops, plus more strawberries on the side, and serve.

When it comes to desserts, apple pie is one of my favorites, both to make and to eat! What is so amazing about this recipe is that it is really easy to make. I prefer to use Granny Smith apples, because they give the filling a great tart flavor, but any tart or semi-tart baking apple (or even a mix of both) will work really well. I also like to use a mix of crisp and soft apples to give the filling more texture. People often think pie crust is hard to make, but this one is easy as pie. There are a few secrets to making light and flaky dough. First, always keep the butter very cold. It's also very important not to handle the dough too much—the warmth of your hands can melt the butter—and to chill the dough before you use it. Also, don't stretch the dough when you place it in the pie pan. I love serving this pie with whipped cream, vanilla ice cream, or even plain or vanilla yogurt, but it's also delicious just by itself. Any way you slice it, this apple pie is a winner!

EASY AS APPLE PIE

PREP TIME: 45 MINUTES (PLUS 30 MINUTES FOR CHILLING) ✕ **COOKING TIME: 60 MINUTES** ✕ **MAKES 1 PIE / SERVES 8 TO 10**

INGREDIENTS

FOR THE PIE DOUGH

2 CUPS (260 g) all-purpose flour

1 TEASPOON fine sea salt

1 CUP (226 g) unsalted butter (2 sticks), chilled

½ CUP (120 ml) ice water, plus more as needed

1 large egg

1 TABLESPOON Demerara or turbinado sugar (optional)

FOR THE FILLING

4 POUNDS (1.8 kg) tart or semi-tart baking apples, peeled, cored, quartered, and cut into ½- to 1-inch (1 to 2.5 cm) cubes

½ CUP (100 g) granulated sugar, plus more as needed

2 TEASPOONS vanilla extract

1 TABLESPOON freshly squeezed lemon juice

½ TEASPOON freshly grated lemon zest

¼ TEASPOON cinnamon (optional)

DIRECTIONS

MAKE THE PIE CRUST

1 In a large bowl or a food processor, combine the flour and salt.

2 Cut the cold butter into small (½-inch / 1.25 cm) cubes. Add the butter to the flour mixture and use a dull knife, a dough cutter, or the pulsing action on the food processor to cut the butter into the flour until it looks like coarse sand.

3 Slowly add the ½ cup (120 ml) of ice water while mixing with the food processor or knife until the dough comes together into a very rough ball. It is all right if there are still some crumbs or if the mixture is not fully dough-like. (If you are using a food processor, you can add the water with the processor running.)

4 Place the dough on a lightly floured work surface and shape it into a disk. Try to handle the dough as little as possible. Wrap the dough in plastic wrap and chill in the refrigerator for at least 30 minutes.

WHILE THE DOUGH IS CHILLING, MAKE THE FILLING:

1 In a large bowl, toss together the apples, granulated sugar, vanilla extract, lemon juice, lemon zest, and cinnamon, if using. If using tart apples, you can add a little more granulated sugar.

NOTE: If you like, you can use 1 teaspoon ground cinnamon instead of the vanilla extract to flavor the pie. You can store the pie for up to a couple days by covering it with foil or a colander (which helps the crust stay crisp) at room temperature.

RECIPE CONTINUES ON FOLLOWING SPREAD

ASSEMBLE AND BAKE THE PIE

1 Preheat the oven to 400°F (200°C).

2 Cut the chilled dough in half. Place 1 piece of dough on a lightly floured work surface; return the other piece to the refrigerator to stay cold. Using a rolling pin, roll out the dough into a 12-inch (30.5 cm) circle. Be sure to roll out the dough from the center outward and to flip the dough over several times while rolling. Lightly flour the work surface and rolling pin as needed to keep the dough from sticking.

3 Carefully roll the circle of dough around the rolling pin and place it in a 9-inch (23 cm) pie pan. Gently lift the edges of the dough, and let them fall into the pan without stretching. There should be about ½-inch (1.25 cm) of dough hanging over the rim of the pie pan.

4 Add the apple mixture to the pie pan, piling the apples slightly higher in the center.

5 Roll out the remaining dough using the instructions from step 2. Using your finger, brush the edge of the dough with a little bit of ice water so it becomes sticky. Carefully roll the dough around the rolling pin and place it on top of the apples with the wet side facing down. There should be about 1 inch (2.5 cm) of dough hanging over the rim of the pie pan. If there is extra dough hanging off the edge, use a knife to cut off the excess. Using your fingers, roll the 1 inch (2.5 cm) of dough hanging off the edge downward and around the bottom crust to form a log-shaped roll around the rim of the pie plate.

6 Using two fingers, gently squeeze and twist the edges of the pie crust to create an up-and-down wavelike pattern all around the pie.

7 Using a knife, cut 4 or 5 (1-inch long / 2.5 cm) slits in the top of the crust. The slits will let steam from the cooking apples escape and keep the crust from bursting while it cooks.

8 If you have time, chill the pie in the refrigerator for 10 to 15 minutes.

9 In a small bowl, whisk the egg with 1 tablespoon of water until the mixture is a uniform yellow color with no streaks of egg white or yolk. Using a pastry brush, brush the egg mixture evenly over the top of the pie. Sprinkle with a thin layer of Demerara or turbinado sugar, if using.

10 Place the pie on a baking sheet and bake for 20 minutes. Rotate the pie front to back then reduce the oven temperature to 350°F (180°C). Continue baking until the crust is golden brown and the filling starts to bubble, 40 to 50 minutes. If the crust is getting too dark, cover the top with aluminum foil and let it finish baking.

11 Remove the pie from the oven, place directly on a wire rack, and let cool for at least 30 minutes. Serve warm or at room temperature.

This is a recipe that my dad taught me. It was passed down from my grandmother and has been changed by each of us. Every weekend my dad and I make this recipe. It has a relatively high ratio of flour to water, so it makes dense and flavorful bread that is perfect for toasting and serving with butter and jam, or to accompany an omelet for a weekend breakfast. In this recipe, the kneading can be done by hand or with a stand mixer. The bread can also be made in one day, or started after dinner and put in the refrigerator overnight to be baked before breakfast. How great is it to wake up to the smell of fresh bread?

BACK TO BASICS BREAD

PREP TIME: 30 MINUTES (BY HAND) ✕ **RISING TIME: 3¼ HOURS (IF MAKING THE SAME DAY)** ✕ **COOKING TIME: 45 MINUTES** ✕
MAKES 2 (9-INCH / 23 CM) LOAVES OF BREAD

INGREDIENTS

1 (¼-ounce / 7 g) package active-dry yeast

2½ **CUPS** plus 2 tablespoons (630 ml) warm water

4¾ **CUPS** (618 g) all-purpose flour

1 **TABLESPOON** kosher salt

2 **CUPS** (260 g) whole wheat flour

¼ **TEASPOON** vegetable or canola oil

1 **TABLESPOON** cornmeal for dusting bottom of bread pans (optional)

ALTERNATIVE

USING A STAND MIXER AND DOUGH HOOK

You can save time by using a stand mixer to knead the dough. Instead of steps 4 and 5, put the sponge, water, salt, and the remaining 4 cups (522 g) of all-purpose flour and the whole wheat flour into a mixing bowl. Attach a dough hook to the mixer and mix the ingredients on low. Once the ingredients are thoroughly mixed, increase the speed to medium and mix until the dough is smooth and elastic as described in step 5. This usually takes about 5 to 10 minutes.

DIRECTIONS

1 Empty the package of yeast into a medium bowl. Add 6 tablespoons (90 ml) of the warm water and ¾ cup (96 g) of the all-purpose flour. With your hands, thoroughly mix the yeast, warm water, and flour and form into a small ball about 2½ inches (6 cm) in diameter. This is the "sponge."

2 Pour the remaining 2¼ cups (540 ml) of warm water into a separate small bowl. With a knife, cut a small "X" into the sponge and gently drop it into the small bowl, being careful not to spill any water. The water should cover the top of the sponge.

3 Add the salt to the medium bowl. When the sponge floats to the surface of the water (usually after 3 to 6 minutes, depending on how active the yeast is), carefully pour the sponge and all the water back into the medium bowl with the salt.

4 Add the remaining 4 cups (522 g) of all-purpose flour and the whole wheat flour to the sponge mixture in the medium bowl and use your hands to thoroughly mix everything together until a dough forms.

5 Empty the dough onto a lightly floured work surface and knead until smooth and elastic with a slightly "tacky" feel, 15 to 20 minutes. I find the best technique for kneading is to stand over the dough and firmly press the heels of your hands into the dough 2 to 3 times in a row, folding it in half after each time. Next, rotate the dough 90 degrees, fold it in half, and repeat. The dough should stick together into a cohesive ball. If the dough splits or cracks after 5 minutes of kneading, that means it's too dry. Fix this by adding water, 1 tablespoon at a time, to the dough and kneading it in. If the dough is too sticky and won't come off your hands, add flour, 1 tablespoon at a time, directly to the dough and knead until the dough has a slightly tacky feel. Form the dough into a ball.

RECIPE CONTINUES ON FOLLOWING SPREAD

ALTERNATIVE

LETTING THE DOUGH RISE OVERNIGHT

One thing I like to do is to make the dough before I go to bed and then bake it for breakfast. You can do this by putting the kneaded, unrisen dough in a lightly oiled bowl, covering the bowl with plastic wrap, and putting the dough in the refrigerator. The next morning, take the dough out of the refrigerator, deflate the dough, and follow the recipe starting from step 8.

6 Put the dough in a clean medium bowl that's been lightly oiled with the vegetable or canola oil. Cover the bowl with a clean, damp tea towel (or plastic wrap). This prevents the dough from getting a hard crust while it rises. Let the dough rise at room temperature for 90 minutes.

7 Remove the towel and use your hands to gently push down on the dough, gradually deflating it. Replace the towel and let the dough rise for another 75 minutes.

8 Gently pull the dough out of the bowl and place it on a clean work surface. With a knife, cut the dough into 2 equal loaves.

9 Lightly oil 2 (9-inch / 23 cm) loaf pans. If you want, sprinkle ½ tablespoon of cornmeal onto the bottom of each pan to give the bread a cornmeal bottom. Lay a loaf in each pan. Cover the pans with the damp tea towel and let the dough rise at room temperature for another 30 minutes. Meanwhile, preheat the oven to 400°F (200°C).

10 With a sharp knife, cut a slit down the length of each loaf. Place the loaves in the oven then carefully throw a handful of ice cubes onto the oven floor and close the door. Bake for 45 minutes.

11 Remove the loaves from the oven then carefully take them out of their pans and let cool. Slice with a serrated knife.

NOTE: Loaves that are not eaten right away, once cooled, can be wrapped in a double layer of plastic bags and frozen for several months.

My grandmother taught me how to make popovers when I was five years old. Popovers look impressive and complicated to make, but are actually very simple—they do all the work themselves! A couple secrets to getting them to "pop" are to make sure the milk is warm and the butter is melted and to not preheat the oven. I especially like "eggy" popovers and love to eat them with butter and jelly or jam. Popovers are a real crowd-pleaser and delicious any way you eat them!

POPOVERS THAT POP!

PREP TIME: 10 TO 15 MINUTES ✕ **COOKING TIME: 30 TO 45 MINUTES** ✕ **MAKES 6 POPOVERS**

INGREDIENTS

1 CUP (240 ml) whole milk (nonfat and low-fat milk can also be used)

1 TABLESPOON salted butter

1 CUP (130 g) all-purpose flour

2 large eggs

NOTE: If you use a 6-cup jumbo muffin tin or popover pan, fill each cup three-quarters full. These pans make bigger popovers than a standard muffin tin. If you use a 12-cup standard muffin tin, fill up as many as you can, usually 6, almost to the top, and put a little water in any empty cups. If you don't have a popover or muffin pan, you can use custard cups or any small 6-ounce (180 ml) baking containers placed on a baking sheet.

DIRECTIONS

1 Generously grease a 6-cup jumbo muffin tin or popover pan with cooking spray or vegetable oil. (You can also use a standard muffin tin; please see note.) Make sure to grease each cup very well, because the batter can stick if you aren't using a well-greased pan. (Alternatively, use a nonstick pan.)

2 In a small heavy-bottomed saucepan, warm the milk and butter over medium heat until the butter is completely melted and the milk is warm, about 2 minutes. (You can also heat the milk and butter together in a microwave for about 60 to 80 seconds using a glass or ceramic bowl.)

3 Pour the heated milk, butter, flour, and eggs into a blender or a stand mixer. Blend the mixture for 90 seconds, first at a low setting then at a medium setting (or on a high setting if using a stand mixer). Occasionally stop the blender and stir the mixture with a spatula to ensure that the flour is thoroughly mixed into the batter. Alternatively, you can mix by hand; beat the mixture vigorously with a whisk for 2 minutes.

4 Pour the batter into the tin until each cup is filled three-quarters full.

5 Place the filled muffin tin in a cool oven and turn the oven on to 400°F (200°C). Do not preheat the oven!

6 Bake until the popovers rise and are golden brown, about 30 to 45 minutes. No peeking! Do not open the oven before 30 minutes.

7 Remove the popovers from the oven and serve immediately. If you aren't ready to eat, turn the oven off, but leave the popovers inside to keep warm until you're ready to serve them.

DEDICATION

To Granny, who gave us our passion for cooking, and to Grandma and Ipa, who are always willing to try what we make.

And to Pop-Pop, who was so supportive of us and will always remain in our hearts.

ACKNOWLEDGMENTS

We would like to thank Holly La Due and Amy Sly, without whom this book could not have happened, and our family, for their constant support throughout this project.

© Prestel Verlag, Munich • London • New York 2019
A member of Verlagsgruppe Random House GmbH
Neumarkter Strasse 28 • 81673 Munich

In respect to links in the book, Verlagsgruppe Random House expressly notes that no illegal content was discernible on the linked sites at the time the links were created. The Publisher has no influence at all over the current and future design, content or authorship of the linked sites. For this reason Verlagsgruppe Random House expressly disassociates itself from all content on linked sites that has been altered since the link was created and assumes no liability for such content.
Text © 2019 Esme Washburn
Photography © 2019 Calista Washburn

Prestel Publishing Ltd.
14-17 Wells Street
London W1T 3PD

Prestel Publishing
900 Broadway, Suite 603
New York, NY 10003

Library of Congress Control Number: 2018947873

A CIP catalogue record for this book is available from the British Library.

Editorial direction: Holly La Due
Design and layout: Amy Sly
Production: Karen Farquhar and Anjali Pala
Copyediting: Lauren Salkeld
Proofreading: Monica Parcell

MIX
Paper from
responsible sources
FSC® C008047
FSC
www.fsc.org

Verlagsgruppe Random House FSC® N001967

Printed and bound in China

ISBN 978-3-7913-8507-5

www.prestel.com

ESME & CALISTA

Esme and Calista Washburn are sisters living in New York City. Esme, who is in middle school, is an amateur chef and cooking enthusiast. She has learned everything she knows about cooking from her grandmother. Calista, a recent high school graduate and budding photographer, loves helping out in the kitchen and eating the delicious food that Esme cooks.

Esme (Age 12)

Calista (Age 17)

Esme (Age 10)

Esme (Age 12)